STATE OF THE ART PROGRAM

# Portfolios

*Robyn Montana Turner*

**BARRETT KENDALL PUBLISHING, Ltd.**

AUSTIN, TEXAS

# CREDITS

## EDITORIAL

**Project Director:** *Linda Dunlap*

**Senior Development Editor:** *Linda Dunlap*

**Editors:** *Melissa Blackwell Burke, Claire Miller Colombo, Kathleen Fitzgibbon, Jody Frank, Mary Ann Frishman, Patty Moynahan, Tara Turner, Anne Walker*

**Copy Editors:** *Kathleen Unger, Sandra Wolfgang*

**Editorial Support:** *Mary Corbett, Elaine Clift Gore, Judy McBurney*

**Administrative Manager:** *Mark Blangger*

**Administrative Support::** *Laurie O'Meara*

## DESIGN, PRODUCTION, AND PHOTO RESEARCH

**Project Director:** *Pun Nio*

**Designers:** *Leslie Kell Designs, Jane Thurmond Designs, Pun Nio*

**Design and Electronic Files:** *Dodson Publication Services, Leslie Kell Designs, Jane Thurmond Designs, Linda Kensicki*

**Photo Research:** *Mark Blangger, Laurie O'Meara*

**Photo Art Director:** *Pun Nio*

**Cover Design:** *Leslie Kell Designs; Art director, Pun Nio; Student Art: Sun, Bees, and Flowers-Calli, Forest Trail Elementary; Dinosaur-James, Woodridge Elementary; Boy-Juan, Zavala Elementary; Pot-Chris, Woodridge Elementary; Mask-Rickey, Our Lady of Perpetual Help; Background-Brushworks Photo Disc.*

Printed in the United States of America

ISBN 1-889105-12-0                    4 5 6 7 8  RD  02 01 00 99

STATE OF THE ART PROGRAM

# Portfolios

## CONSULTANTS

**Doug Blandy, Ph.D.**
*Associate Professor*
Program in Arts and Administration
University of Oregon
Eugene, Oregon

**Cindy G. Broderick, Ph.D.**
*Art Faculty*
Alamo Heights Junior School
Alamo Heights Independent School District
San Antonio, Texas

**Sara Chapman, M.A.**
*Visual Arts Coordinator*
Alief Independent School District
Houston, Texas

**Brenda J. Chappell, Ph.D.**
*Art Consultant*
Tennessee State University
Department of Art
Nashville, Tennessee

**James Clarke, M.A.**
*Program Director for Visual Arts and
Elementary Creative Drama*
Aldine Independent School District
Houston, Texas

**Georgia Collins, Ph.D.**
*Professor, Department of Art*
University of Kentucky
Lexington, Kentucky

**Gloria Contreras, Ph.D.**
*Professor, Department of Teacher
Education and Administration*
University of North Texas
Denton, Texas

**Sandra M. Epps, Ph.D.**
*Director, Multicultural Programs*
Community School District Five
New York, New York

**Diane C. Gregory, Ph.D.**
*Associate Professor of Art Education
Department of Art and Design*
Southwest Texas State University
San Marcos, Texas

**Susan M. Mayer, M.A.**
*Coordinator of Museum Education
Senior Lecturer of Art*
The University of Texas at Austin
Austin, Texas

**Aaronetta Hamilton Pierce**
*Consultant, African American Art and Artists*
San Antonio, Texas

**Renee Sandell, Ph.D.**
*Professor, Department of Art Education*
Maryland Institute, College of Art
Baltimore, Maryland

# CONTRIBUTING WRITERS

**Pamela Geiger Stephens, Ph.D.**
*Art Education Consultant*
Colleyville, Texas

**Sharon Warwick, M.Ed., M.S.A.**
*Art Specialist*
Central Junior High School
Euless, Texas
Tarrant County Junior College
Hurst, Texas

**Kay K. Wilson, M.A.**
*Art Specialist*
North Texas Institute for Educators
on the Visual Arts
University of North Texas
Denton, Texas

# REVIEWERS

**Gini Robertson-Baker**
*Classroom Teacher*
Bivins Elementary School
Amarillo Independent School District
Amarillo, Texas

**Mary Cavaioli**
*Art Educator*
Bay View Elementary School
Broward County Schools
Fort Lauderdale, Florida

**Rosalinda Champion**
*Art Specialist*
Edinburg Senior High School
Edinburg Consolidated School District
Edinburg, Texas

**Deborah Cooper**
*Visual Arts Specialist*
Charlotte-Mecklenburg Schools
Charlotte, North Carolina

**Nancy Mayeda**
*Principal, Creative Fine Arts Magnet School*
San Francisco Unified School District
San Francisco, California

**Kathie McBride**
*Art Specialist*
The Buckley School
Sherman Oaks, California

**Jerilyn Tate**
*Classroom Teacher*
Marion Primary School
Smyth County Schools
Marion, Virginia

**Marilyn Wylie**
*Art Specialist*
Conley Elementary School
Aldine Independent School District
Houston, Texas

iv

# Portfolios

# CONTENTS

# Unit 1

# Art in Your Life

# Art in Many Places

# Unit 3

# Many Types of Art

# Ways of Expressing

# Unit 5

# Sizes of Artworks

# More Ways of Making Artworks

Gabriele Münter. (Detail) *Schnee und Sonne (Snow and Sun)*, 1911. Oil on cardboard, 20 by 27 ½ inches. The University of Iowa Museum of Art, Iowa City. Gift of Owen and Leone Elliott. 1968.63.

# Art in Your Life

Art is all around you.
It is in your life.
Look for it in the lines of your fingerprint.
Find it in the shapes of family faces.
Discover it in the colors
of your neighborhood.

Look, find, and discover.
Where will you begin?

## First Look

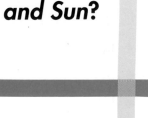

This is a faraway neighborhood.
Why did the artist name her picture *Snow and Sun*?
How does the picture make you feel?

**Lesson 1**

# Lines and Shapes Around You

**A**

**B** Connie, Liestman Elementary. *Doggin' It.* Marker, tempera cakes, 18 by 20 inches.

**C**

You can discover **lines** in your world.
Look for lines in these pictures.
Can you find
- straight lines near curved ones?
- wavy lines on water?
- lines to use for hopscotch?

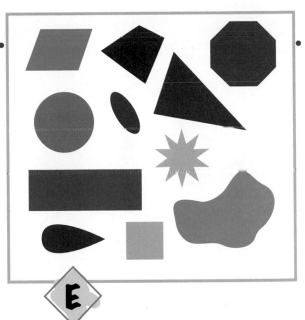

D

E

Joni, Forest Trail Elementary. *Beary Rock.* Crayon, neon tempera, marker on paper, 18 by 12 inches.

Lines often make **shapes.**
Look at the pictures again.
Where do you see a circle?
Point to a square and a triangle.
Look for some shapes of people.
Which other shapes can you find?

# Seeing Like an Artist

I can see lines and shapes.
They are all around me.
I could draw some of them.
I could make a sketchbook.
My teacher can show me how to make it.

*Lines and Shapes Around You*

 Elizabeth Catlett. *Baile (Dance)*, 1970. Lino-cut, 16 by 30 inches. © 1996
Elizabeth Catlett/Licensed by VAGA, New York.

# Neighborhood Friends

Neighbors live near each other.
Many of them are friends.
They work and play together.
Artists show neighborhood friends.

What is happening in **A**?
How does the artist show **movement**?
Do you think the children are friends?
Tell why.

Marie Bashkirtseff. *The Meeting*, 1884. Oil on canvas, 74¹⁵/₁₆ by 68¹⁵/₁₆ inches. Musée d'Orsay, Paris, France. Giraudon/Art Resource, New York.

What does it mean to be a friend?
Look at the lines and shapes in **B**.
What is the group of friends doing?
Is someone left out of the group?
What do you think the artist was saying?

# Try Your Hand

Who are your friends?
Do they live in your neighborhood?
1. Draw a picture of you and them playing.
2. Show some movement.
What will you be doing in the picture?

# Color and Texture Around You

The world is filled with **colors.**
How many colors can you see?
Name some colors in the pictures.
Artists use many colors.

Artists use **texture**, too.
You can feel a rough or smooth texture.
It can be soft or hard.
You can see a shiny or dull texture.

What is the dog's texture?
Does the dog fill most of the **space**?
Explain.

Frank Romero. *Toto*, 1984. Oil on canvas, 32 by 60 inches. © 1984 by Frank Romero. Photograph by Douglas M. Parker.

**C**

Peter, Forest Trail Elementary. *Smiling Sun.* Crayon, glitter paint, tempera on paper, 18 by 12 inches.

Wash it.

Wipe it.

Blot it.

Go to another color.

The artist used a brush and paints to make **B**.
This picture is called a **painting.**
Where do you see **brush strokes**?
Brush strokes make texture with lines, shapes, and colors.

## Planning Like an Artist

I can plan to paint a picture.
It could have texture.
It could show brush strokes.
Which colors shall I plan to use?

 Carmen Lomas Garza. *Sandía/Watermelon*, 1986. Gouache painting, 20 by 28 inches. Collection of Dudley D. Brooks and Tomas Ybarra-Frausto, New York. © 1986 Carmen Lomas Garza. Photograph by Wolfgang Dietze.

# Neighborhood Families

Families can be friends and relatives.
They work and play together.
Artists paint pictures of neighborhood families.

What is happening in **A**?
What ages are the family members?
Point to something shiny.
Suppose that you could touch things in **A**.
How would each thing feel?

Palmer C. Hayden. *Midsummer Night in Harlem*, 1938. Oil on canvas, 25 by 30 inches. Palmer C. Hayden Collection. Gift of Miriam A. Hayden. The Museum of African American Art, Los Angeles.

Now look at **B** and **C**.
What are the families doing?
What ages are the family members?
How do these paintings of evening gatherings make you feel?

 **Try Your Hand**

1. Paint a picture of your family.
2. Show your neighborhood.
Will your brush strokes show texture?
Which colors will you use?

 Kecia, Amelia Earhart Learning Center. *My Family Together.* Crayon on paper, 18 by 12 inches.

*Color and Texture Around You*  **9**

# Colors in Your World

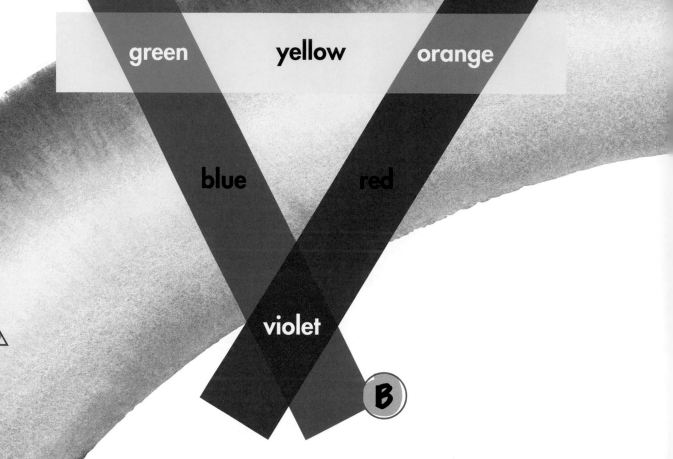

green     yellow     orange

blue     red

violet

Ⓐ

Ⓑ

Look at the color bars in **B**.
They show groups of colors.
**Primary colors** belong to a group.
They are yellow, **red**, and **blue**.

Yellow and **red** together make orange.
Orange is a **secondary color.**
Point to the group of secondary colors.
What colors can you mix to make them?

Marc Chagall.
*The Red Rooster*,
1940. Oil on
canvas, 28¾ by
36 inches.
Cincinnati Art
Museum,
bequest of Mary
E. Johnston.
1967.1426.

Now look at **C**.
What primary color did the artist use?
Point to a secondary color.

What is unusual about **C**?
Do you think the scene is **imaginary**?

## Thinking Like an Artist

**I wonder how artists choose their colors.**
**What happens when I mix colors?**
**My favorite colors are . . . .**

Vincent van Gogh.
*Flowering Garden*, 1888.
Oil on canvas, 28¾ by
36¼ inches. Private collec-
tion, Zurich, Switzerland.
On loan at Metropolitan
Museum of Art, New York.
Giraudon Art Resource,
New York.

# Neighborhood Gardens

Where is your favorite garden?
Who takes care of it?
Artists like to show neighborhood gardens.

Yellow, orange, and red are **warm colors.**
Does **A** or **B** show warm colors?
Violet, blue, and green are **cool colors.**
Does **A** or **B** show cool colors?
How does each picture make you feel?

C

Beatrice, Forest Trail Elementary.
*Garden Party.* Watered tempera,
crayon, glitter crayon, 12 by 18 inches.

B

Claude Oscar Monet. *Bridge over a Pool of Water Lilies*,
1899. Oil on canvas, 36½ by 29 inches. The Metropolitan
Museum of Art. H. O. Havemeyer Collection. Bequest of
Mrs. H. O. Havemeyer, 1929. 29.100.113.

Artists put light colors next to dark ones.
This helps the shapes stand out clearly.
Point to light colors and dark colors in **A**, **B**, and **C**.

## Try Your Hand

Imagine a beautiful garden.
What shapes and colors will you use?
1. Draw a picture with oil pastels.
2. Choose warm or cool colors.
3. Brush some thinned paint over it.

# PORTFOLIO PROJECT

## My Neighborhood

What is special about your neighborhood?
Who is special in it?

### 1. Cut away a side from a box.

### 2. Use cool colors.
Paint buildings and plants.

### 3. Use warm colors.
Draw people and animals.

### 4. Make your drawings stand up.

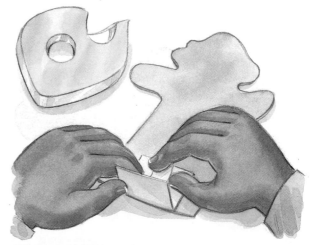

How do the warm and cool colors look together?
Do you like your neighborhood artwork?
What is your favorite part?

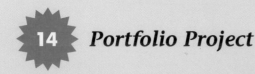

 Jennifer, Conley Elementary. *The City Park.* Cardboard, tempera, marker, 14 by 5 by 5 inches.

 Charles, Conley Elementary. *Sport City.* Cardboard, tempera, marker, 14 by 5 by 5 inches.

Wassily Kandinsky. *Lady (Portrait of Gabriele Münter),* ca. 1910. Oil on canvas, 44 by 43½ inches. Munich, Lenbachhaus. Photograph by AKG London.

Gabriele Münter. *Schnee und Sonne (Snow and Sun),* 1911. Oil on cardboard, 20 by 27½ inches. The University of Iowa Museum of Art, Iowa City. Gift of Owen and Leone Elliott. 1968.63.

The artist in **A** painted **B**.
She belonged to a group of artists.
They liked to use bold, bright colors.
They lived in a village far away.
Some of her paintings show the village.

Look at the colors in **B**.
Point to cool colors.
Point to warm colors.
How does the title go with the colors?
How does the person in the picture feel?

C Stuart Davis. *Swing Landscape*, 1938. Oil on canvas, 88 by 176 inches. Indiana University Art Museum, Bloomington. © 1998 Estate of Stuart Davis/Licensed by VAGA, New York. Photograph by Michael Cavanagh, Kevin Montague.

Point out the primary colors in **C**.
Now find the secondary colors.
Find straight and curved lines.
Point to five different shapes.
Would the shapes in **C** look good in **B**?
Explain.

What is the same about **B** and **C**?
What is different?
What do you think each artist was saying?
Would you like to see **B** in a museum? Explain.
Would you like to hang **C** on your wall?
Tell why or why not.

# WRITE ABOUT ART

Look again at **B** on page 16.
It shows a town on a bright winter day.

Imagine that you are a visitor to this town.
Write a postcard to a friend.
Tell what you have seen.

**Make a postcard from a piece of paper.**

Draw a picture on one side of the paper.

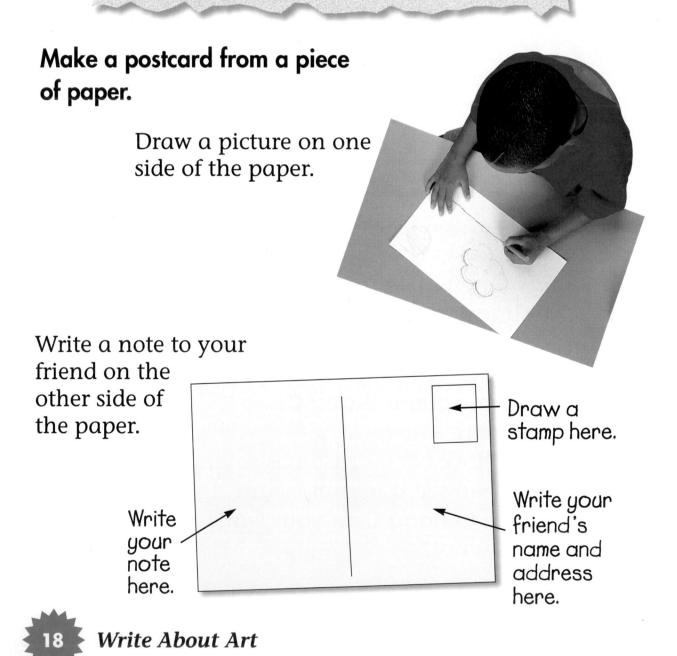

Write a note to your friend on the other side of the paper.

Draw a stamp here.

Write your note here.

Write your friend's name and address here.

# What Have You Learned?

Where have you seen these pictures?

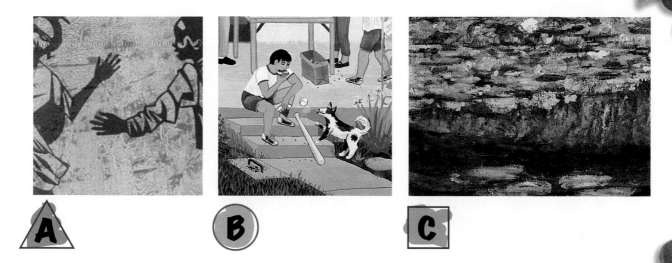

**A**      **B**      **C**

1. Point to curved lines.
2. Name other types of lines in the pictures.
3. Where do you see triangles?
4. Point to shapes of flowers.

5. Which pictures show something with a soft texture?
6. Point to something with a shiny texture.
7. Which pictures show primary colors?
8. Point to some warm colors and cool colors.

9. Did you have a favorite activity? Explain.
10. What else did you learn about art in your life?

Elizabeth Catlett. (Detail) *Baile (Dance)*, 1970. Lino-cut, 16 by 30 inches. © 1996 Elizabeth Catlett/Licensed by VAGA, New York.

Carmen Lomas Garza. (Detail) *Sandía/Watermelon*, 1986. Gouache painting, 20 by 28 inches. Collection of Dudley D. Brooks and Tomas Ybarra-Frausto, New York. © 1986 Carmen Lomas Garza. Photograph by Wolfgang Dietze.

Claude Oscar Monet. (Detail) *Bridge over a Pool of Water Lilies*, 1899. Oil on canvas, 36½ by 29 inches. The Metropolitan Museum of Art. H. O. Havemeyer Collection. Bequest of Mrs. H. O. Havemeyer, 1929. 29.100.113.

Katsushika Hokusai. (Detail) *Paysans lavant leur cheval sous la cascade Yoshitsune (The Yoshitsune Horse-Washing Waterfall)*, ca. 1831-1832. Woodcut, 15 by 10 inches. Collection of the Montreal Museum of Fine Arts, Purchase, John W. Tempest Fund. Photograph by Christine Guest, MBAM/MMFA.

# Art in Many Places

Art is all over the world.
It is faraway and nearby.
It is on the land and in the sky.

Look around you.
See the lines, shapes, colors,
and textures.
Remember something beautiful.
Imagine things you've never seen.

Where is art?
You can find it in many places.
Just look, remember, and imagine.

## First Look

**What is happening in the picture?**
**Where is the horse?**
**Do you think the horse likes what is going on?**
**Explain.**

# Patterns of Lines, Shapes, and Colors

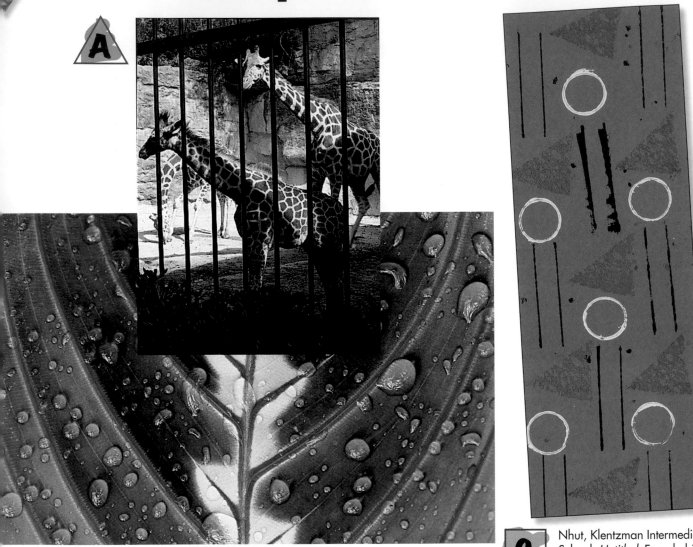

**A**

**B**

**C** Nhut, Klentzman Intermediate School. *Untitled.* Found objects, tempera on construction paper, 6 by 18 inches.

**Patterns** are repeated lines, shapes, and colors.
Look at the patterns in these pictures.
Find the repeated lines, shapes, and colors.

Artists show many kinds of patterns.
Point to the pattern you like best.

# How to
## Print Patterns

1. Find objects to use for printing.

2. Press an object in the paint.

TEMPERA

3. Press on the paper. Lift.

4. Press again.

Artists make **prints** in many ways.
They can create printed patterns.
Which picture shows a print?

# Seeing Like an Artist

I can see patterns all around me.
They are in the trees.
They are in my classroom.
They are even on my fingers!

*Patterns of Lines, Shapes, and Colors*  23

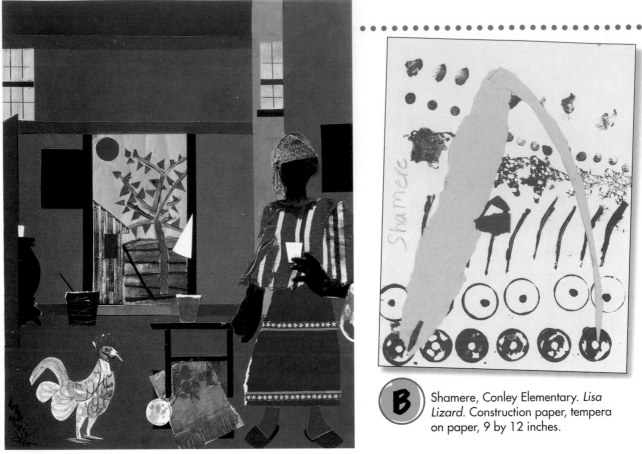

Romare Bearden. *Morning of the Rooster*, 1980. Collage on board, 18 by 13¾ inches. Courtesy Estate of Romare Bearden/ACA Galleries New York, Munich.

**B** Shamere, Conley Elementary. *Lisa Lizard*. Construction paper, tempera on paper, 9 by 12 inches.

# Animals in Neighborhoods

Artists show animals in neighborhoods.
They show them in different ways.
Which animals are in your neighborhood?

Look at **A**.
It is a **collage.**
The shapes are cut or torn from paper.
Then they are pasted down.
Which animal is in this collage?
What patterns do you see?

*Lesson 4*

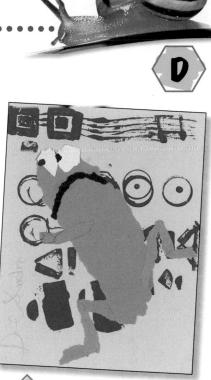

C

Henri Matisse. *The Snail*, 1953. Gouache on paper, 112¾ by 113 inches. The Tate Gallery, London. Art Resource, New York.

E

DeAndre, Conley Elementary. *Fred Frog.* Construction paper, tempera on paper, 9 by 12 inches.

Point to other collages.
Name the animals you see.
Which animals look real?
Which ones look imaginary?

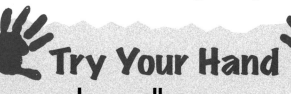

# Try Your Hand

You can make a collage.
Which animal will you show?
1. Look back on page 23.
2. Print some patterns for a background.
3. Let them dry.
4. Cut or tear some shapes for an animal.
5. Glue them onto the background.
Do you like your collage?

*Patterns of Lines, Shapes, and Colors*

# Shapes of Faces

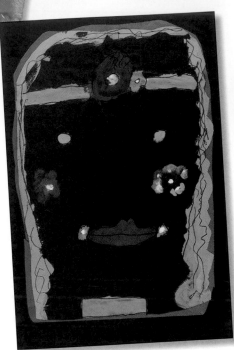

Mary, Forest Trail
Elementary. *African
Blossom.* Construction
paper, tempera,
marker, 12 by 18
inches.

Faces come in many sizes and shapes.
Faces **express,** or show, feelings.
Each face is different.
How is your face different from others?

Look at the faces in the pictures.
Draw around their shapes with your finger.
How are they different?
Which expressions do they show?

Paul Klee. *Senecio,* 1922. Oil on gauze on cardboard, 16 by 15 inches. Oeffentliche Kunstsammlung Basel, Kunstmuseum. Photograph by Oeffentliche Kunstsammlung Basel, Martin Bühler.

Look closely at **D**.
What do you notice about the eyes?
What else is different about the face?
What do you think the artist was saying?

# Planning Like an Artist

I can plan to study faces.
They have different sizes and shapes.
Sometimes they express feelings.
I can draw faces in my sketchbook.
Each one will be special.

Laura Wheeler Waring. *Frankie (or Portrait of a Child)*, 1937. The National Archives, Washington, D. C., Harmon Foundation Collection.

B Rebecca, Hill Elementary. *Self-portrait.* Black glue, oil pastels on construction paper, 12 by 14 inches.

# People in Neighborhoods

The pictures on these pages are called **portraits.**
They show likenesses of real people.
The artist of **C** painted a portrait of her son.
He was her **model.**
Point to other models on these pages.

Alice Neel. *Richard at Age Five*, 1944. Oil on canvas, 26 by 14 inches. © The Estate of Alice Neel. Courtesy Robert Miller Gallery, New York.

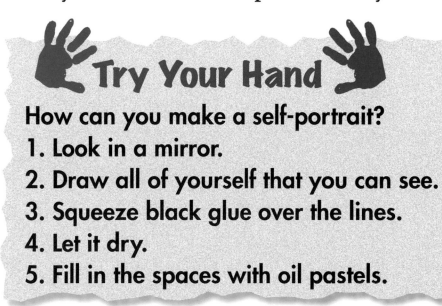 Kristi, Hill Elementary. *Self-portrait.* Black glue, oil pastels on construction paper, 14 by 12 inches.

Pictures **B** and **D** are **self-portraits.**
The artists created likenesses of themselves.
Have you ever made a portrait of yourself?

## Try Your Hand

**How can you make a self-portrait?**
1. Look in a mirror.
2. Draw all of yourself that you can see.
3. Squeeze black glue over the lines.
4. Let it dry.
5. Fill in the spaces with oil pastels.

*Shapes of Faces*  **29**

# Forms in Places

**Architects** are artists who plan buildings.
They make small **models** of their plans.
Some architects design art museums.
You can visit art museums to see artworks.
Which pictures show art museums?

**B** Philip Johnson (architect). Art Museum of South Texas, Corpus Christi, Texas.

**Architecture** is made of **forms.**
You can go around a form.
Point to forms in the pictures.

**c**

sphere

cone

cylinder

cube

# Thinking Like an Artist

I can think like an architect.
I can plan buildings with forms.
I can make models of my plans.
Maybe I'll draw some plans
for an art museum.
I can use my sketchbook.

## Playscapes in Neighborhoods

Some architects plan **playscapes.**
They design safe and fun places to play.
Many playscapes are in parks.
Where is your favorite playscape?
What makes it special?

# How to
## Make a Playscape Model

1. Cut and tear some shapes.

2. Bend them. Fold them. Tape and glue them to make forms.

Laura, Hill Elementary. *Playscape*. Poster board, construction paper, 11¾ by 9½ by 4 inches.

3. Arrange your forms as a playscape.

4. Glue or paste them onto a base.

## Try Your Hand

Imagine the best playscape in the world. How would it look?

1. Make a model with paper.
2. Cut, fold, bend, and paste.
3. Use your imagination.

Will the playscape be in your neighborhood?

*Forms in Places*

## Making an Animal Stamp Print

Which animal will you choose?
Will it be real or imaginary?

1. Make a **printing plate.**

2. Press hard to draw an animal. Draw some patterns.

3. Tape a handle onto the back.

4. Press the plate onto paint.

5. Make a print.

6. Add more patterns to the plate. Make another print.

How many prints did you make?
Did you change your printing plate?
Are you pleased with your work? Why?

# PORTFOLIO GALLERY

 Raul, Zavala Elementary. *Untitled*. Water-based ink, construction paper, 12 by 9 inches.

 Pablo, Zavala Elementary. *Untitled*. Tempera, construction paper, 12 by 9 inches.

# TALK ABOUT ART

Attributed to Katsushika Hokusai. *Untitled* (Believed to be a self-portrait of Katsushika Hokusai), 1900. Reproduced and published by Bunshichi Kobayashi. Woodcut print from original drawing, 23 ⅔ by 10 inches. Sumida City Tokyo, Peter Morse Collection.

**B**

Katsushika Hokusai. *Paysans lavant leur cheval sous la cascade Yoshitsune (The Yoshitsune Horse-Washing Waterfall)*, ca. 1831-1832. Woodcut, 15 by 10 inches. Collection of the Montreal Museum of Fine Arts, Purchase, John W. Tempest Fund. Photograph by Christine Guest, MBAM/MMFA.

Picture **A** shows a portrait of an artist.
He lived across the ocean.
What can you tell about him?

The artist in **A** made **B**.
He used colored ink and a block of wood to print **B**.

 Melissa W. Miller. *Flood*, 1983. Oil on linen, 59 by 95 inches. Collection, Museum of Fine Arts, Houston. Photograph by Bill Kennedy.

Which animals are in **C**?
What is happening in the painting?
Point to warm and cool colors.

Now look at **B** and **C**.
Where do you see patterns?
How does each picture show movement?
Which picture shows stormy weather?
What was each artist expressing?
Would you like to show **B** to your family? Explain.
Would you like to hang **C** on your wall?
Tell why or why not.

# WRITE ABOUT ART

Look again at **B** on page 36. It shows two men and a horse near a waterfall. The men are washing the horse.

Write a story about the picture.
Your story should have a beginning,
a middle, and an end.
Use these ideas or your own.

### Beginning

Tell how the horse became dirty.

### Middle

Tell how the men found the horse and washed it.

### End

Tell what happened next.

# What Have You Learned?

Where have you seen these pictures?

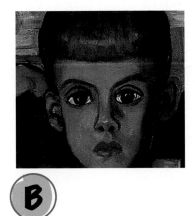

**A**    **B**    **C**

1. Which picture shows a collage?
2. Which picture shows a playscape?
3. Which picture shows a portrait?

4. Point to a work designed by an architect.
5. Which picture shows form?

6. Are the boy's eyes small or large in **B**?
7. What was the artist trying to express?

8. Which picture shows colorful shapes?
9. Which pictures seem playful?

10. Turn back to your favorite artwork. Tell why you like it.
11. Which activity did you like best?
12. What else did you learn about art in many places?

*Art in Many Places*

Henry Moore. *Family Group*, 1951. Bronze, 59¼ by 26½ inches. © Boltin Picture Library, Croton-on-Hudson, New York.

**40** *Unit 3*

# Many Types of Art

Art comes in many sizes, shapes, and forms.
Some artworks are old.
Others are new.
Some are made to be seen but not used.
Others are made to be used as
well as seen.
Some artworks help people think
about what is important to them.
Others can make you laugh.

How many types of art
have you seen?

 **First Look**

**What is this artwork about?**
**What is unusual about it?**
**How does it make you feel?**

# Many Types of Forms

Artist unknown. *Mayan Man and Woman*, ca. 700 A.D. Buff clay with traces of color, 10½ by 5¾ by 3⅞ inches. Honolulu Academy of Arts Purchase, Charles Alfred Castle Memorial Fund, 1973. Photograph by Shuzo Uemoto.

You have learned about architecture.
**Sculpture** is another type of form.
You could go around the sculptures on these pages.

Look at the people in **A**.
Their forms show **positive space.**
The area around them is **negative space.**

The artist of **A** lived in Mexico long ago.
How do you think the man and woman feel about each other?
Explain why you think so.

Artist unknown. *Seated Buddha,* early 8th century, T'ang Dynasty. Gilt bronze, height 8 inches. The Metropolitan Museum of Art, Rogers Fund, 1943. (43.24.3) © 1995 by The Metropolitan Museum of Art.

The artist of **B** lived in China long ago.
This sculpture is about as old as **A**.
The artist made it to help people think about their religion.
Point to the positive space in **B**.
Point to the negative space.

What do you like about **A**?
What do you like about **B**?

## Seeing Like an Artist

My hand is a positive space.
I can find negative space, too.
All I have to do is spread my fingers.

*Many Types of Forms* 43

James Surls. *Once I Saw a Spotted Lady Whose Belly Was Round Like a Ball*, 1974. Wood and wool sculpture, 46¾ by 27½ by 26½ inches. © 1998 James Surls/Licensed by VAGA, New York, NY/Marlborough Gallery, New York. Photograph © 1998 Dallas Museum of Art, General Acquisitions Fund.

# Forms for Fun

The artist in **A** made his child laugh. How did the **sculptor** use his sense of humor in **B**?

Point to the positive space in **B**. Where is the negative space?

Forrest, Woodridge Elementary. *Untitled*. Tempera paint, craft sticks, spools, wooden platform, 5½ by 8½ by 5 inches.

The sculptures on these pages are called **assemblages.**
The sculptors put them together using wood and glue.

Isaac Smith. *Polar Bear*, 1994. Painted wood, plaster, 22 by 49 by 22 inches. Collection of Dr. Kurt Gitter and Alice Rae Yelen.

The artist of **D** is **self-taught.**
He taught himself to draw, paint, and make sculptures.
He makes forms of tigers, fish, birds, and bears.
What do you notice first about **D**?

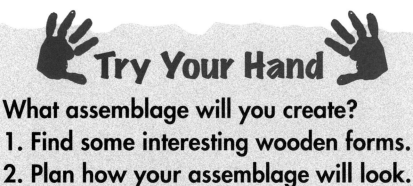

## Try Your Hand

What assemblage will you create?
1. Find some interesting wooden forms.
2. Plan how your assemblage will look.
3. Glue the forms together.
4. Let them dry.
5. Paint your assemblage and add details.
Does your assemblage make people smile?

*Many Types of Forms*

# Forms for Play

People around the world like to play.
Some artists make forms for play.

The sculpture in **A** was made far away.
Point to patterns on the toy horse.
What did the artist use to make **A**?

Artist unknown. *Horse Toy*, ca. 1960. Painted wood, height 10 inches. From the Girard Foundation Collection in the Museum of International Folk Art, a unit of the Museum of New Mexico, Santa Fe, N. Mex. Photograph by Michel Monteaux.

Artist unknown.
*Hand Puppets*,
early 19th century.
Painted wood,
height 16 inches.
From the Girard
Foundation
Collection in the
Museum of
International Folk
Art, a unit of the
Museum of New
Mexico, Santa Fe,
N. Mex.
Photograph by
Michel Monteaux.

The **puppets** in **B** are made of wood, too.
They are about 100 years old.
People performed puppet shows with them.

All of these toys were made to be used.
Each toy is about as tall as your book.
Who do you think played with them?

## Planning Like an Artist

Artists use their imaginations to make toys.
I can use mine, too.
Maybe I'll make some sketches of toys.
They will show my new ideas.

Artist unknown. Acoma Polychrome Jar, ca. 1900. Burnished cream slip, diameter 13 inches. © 1993 Sotheby's, Inc.

Lucy Leuppe McKelvey. *Whirling Rainbow Goddesses*, 1988. Ceramic container, 6¾ by 12 inches. Photograph © by Jerry Jacka.

## Forms to Use

Artists who make **pottery** are called **potters.**
They work with **clay** from the earth.
They create sculpture by hand.

The potter who made **A** lived about 100 years ago.
Later, this way of making pottery was lost.
Potters today are discovering again how to make pots like this one.

Now look at the lines and shapes in **B**.
The potter painted **designs** that show movement.
How are the designs in **B** different from those in **A**?

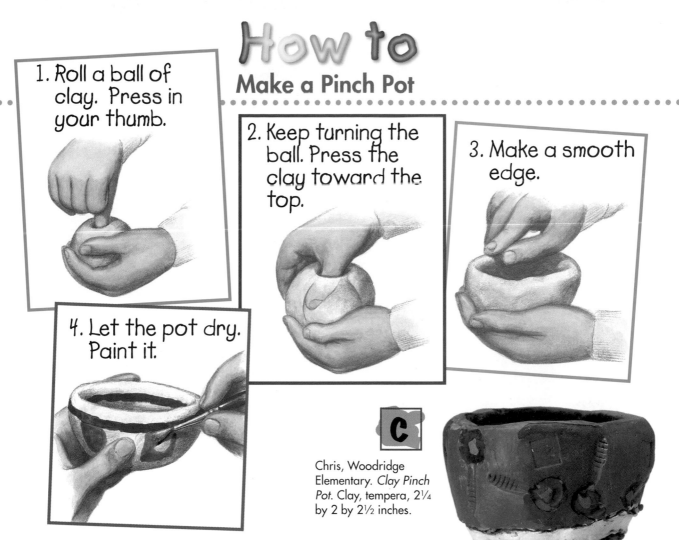

# How to
**Make a Pinch Pot**

1. Roll a ball of clay. Press in your thumb.

2. Keep turning the ball. Press the clay toward the top.

3. Make a smooth edge.

4. Let the pot dry. Paint it.

**C**

Chris, Woodridge Elementary. *Clay Pinch Pot.* Clay, tempera, 2¼ by 2 by 2½ inches.

Clay comes from the earth.
Damp clay is soft.
It gets hard when it dries.
The dry clay is fired in a special oven called a **kiln.**
Then the potter paints it and fires it again.

**D** Catherine, Woodridge Elementary. *Clay Pinch Pot.* Clay, tempera, 3¼ by 2 by 2¼ inches.

# Try Your Hand

1. Make a pinch pot.
2. Carve some textures on it.
3. Paint some designs.
Will you make a lid for your pinch pot?

# Types of Balance

**A**

Artist unknown.
*Double-Headed
Serpent,* 15th cen-
tury. Turquoise
mosaic, 17½
inches. © The
British Museum,
London.

What do you see in **A**?
The sculpture is covered with a **mosaic.**
Small pieces of stone are placed side by side.
They are set into cement.
An artist in Mexico made the sculpture long ago.
It is a symbol for strength and wisdom there.

The pictures on these pages show types of **balance.**
Picture **A** shows **symmetrical balance.**
The sculpture looks the same on both sides.

 **B** Star of Texas Ferris Wheel, Dallas, Texas.

 **C** Doug, Martin Elementary. *Open Flower*. Glue, oil pastels on paper, 18 by 12 inches.

**Radial balance** looks like a wheel or a flower. The lines and shapes go out from the center. Which pictures show radial balance?

# Thinking Like an Artist

Many things in my classroom show balance.
Which ones show symmetrical balance?
Which ones show radial balance?
I can draw them in my sketchbook.
I could make a page for each one.

Amado Peña. *Los Pescados Peña*, 1978. Serigraph, 22 by 32 inches. Courtesy of the artist.

**A**

# Printing Your Way

An artist planned the shapes in **A**.
He made **stencils** to print them.
Are the fish real or imaginary?
Which one do you like best? Why?

A student made an
imaginary animal in **B**.
He printed designs
with his stencils.

James, Woodridge Elementary.
*Untitled*. Tempera, crayon on
paper, 12 by 18 inches

**B**

# How to
## Make a Stencil Print

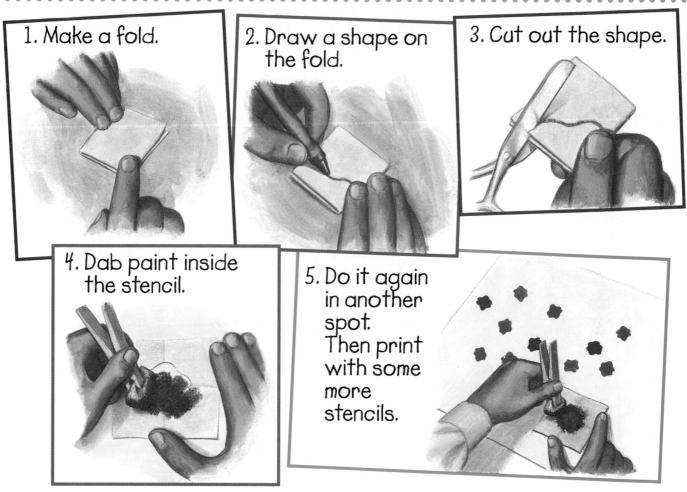

1. Make a fold.

2. Draw a shape on the fold.

3. Cut out the shape.

4. Dab paint inside the stencil.

5. Do it again in another spot. Then print with some more stencils.

You can print designs with a stencil.
Your stencil could help you make patterns, too.

## Try Your Hand

1. Draw a large animal on a large sheet of paper.
2. Make some symmetrical stencils.
3. Print stencil designs all over the animal shape.
4. Use oil pastels to color the space outside your animal.

## Making a Thumbprint Pot

How many ways can you use a new clay pot?

1. Roll some balls of clay.

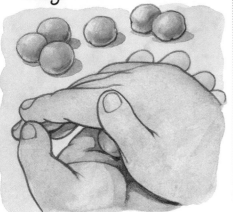

2. Wrap a can in damp paper towels.

3. Make a flat clay bottom for your pot. Press the balls next to each other.

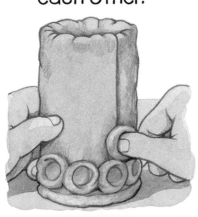

4. Before your pot dries, slide it away carefully.

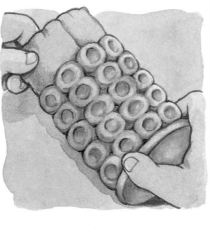

5. Let it dry. Paint it.

Did you have any problems? Explain.
How will you use your new pot?

# PORTFOLIO GALLERY

Elizabeth, Woodridge Elementary. *Thumb-print Jar.* Clay, tempera, 4 by 3 by 4¼ inches.

James, Woodridge Elementary. *Thumb-print Jar.* Clay, tempera, 4 by 2¾ by 3¼ inches.

*Portfolio Gallery*  55

# TALK ABOUT ART

Henry Moore. *Family Group*, 1951. Bronze, 59¼ by 26½ inches. © Boltin Picture Library, Croton-on-Hudson, New York.

The artist in **A** sculpted **B**.
His home was in England.
He studied artworks from Africa and Mexico.

Look at **B**.
What textures do you see?
Point to the positive space.
Point to the negative space.
The artist designed the sculpture for a schoolyard.
Why do you think people liked to gather around it?
Why are the arms joined together?

Barbara Hepworth. *Figure for Landscape*, 1960 (cast 1965). Bronze, 106½ by 53⅞ by 28⅜ inches. Hirshhorn Museum and Sculpture Garden, Smithsonian Institution, Washington, D.C. Gift of Joseph H. Hirshhorn, 1966. Photograph by Lee Stalsworth. 66.2450.

The artist of **C** lived in England, too.
What is going on in her sculpture?
Point to the positive space.
Point to the negative space.

What is alike and different about the sculptures?
What do you think each artist was saying?
Would you like to have **B** in your schoolyard?
Explain.
Would you like to show **C** to your family?
Tell why or why not.

# WRITE ABOUT ART

Look again at the sculpture called *Family Group* on page 56.

**Write a story about a family. Make the people seem real.**

## Remember:

- Tell who is in the story. Use a name for each important person in the story.
- Tell where the story happens.
- Is there a problem? How does it get solved?
- Give your story a beginning, a middle, and an end.

# What Have You Learned?

Where have you seen these pictures?

**A**  **B**  **C**

1. Which picture shows a mosaic?
2. Point to the negative space in **C**.
3. How many round forms can you find?
4. Which pictures show patterns?

5. What type of balance does the wheel in **B** show?
6. Which artwork is designed for movement?
7. Point to an assemblage.
8. Which two sculptures are made of wood?
9. Which sculpture do you like best? Tell why.

10. Turn back to the artwork you would like to learn more about. Tell why.
11. Which was your favorite activity? Why?
12. What else did you learn about the many types of art?

*Many Types of Art*  **59**

William H. Johnson. *Jitterbugs I*, ca. 1940-1941. Oil on plywood, 39¾ by 31¼ inches.
National Museum of American Art, Washington, D. C./Art Resource, New York.

# Ways of Expressing

Artists like to show, or express, feelings and ideas. Their artworks are expressions of their feelings and ideas.

Can you imagine a world without expression?
Who would make music?
Who would dance for you?
Who would write poetry for you to enjoy?
Who would act in a play?
Who would paint pictures for you to see?

People express themselves in many ways. How do you like to express yourself?

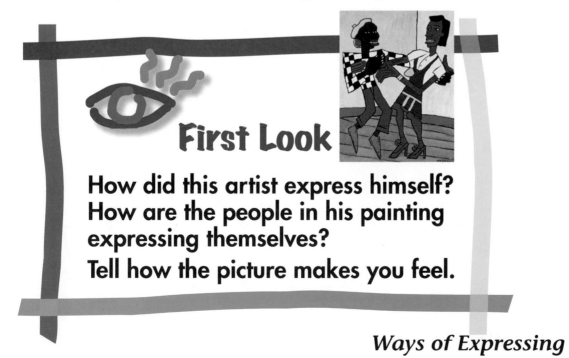

**First Look**

How did this artist express himself?
How are the people in his painting expressing themselves?
Tell how the picture makes you feel.

# Visual Arts

**A**

**B**

**Art** is a small word with a big meaning.
It can mean many things.
Music is a type of art.
Dancing and poetry are, too.
Theater, storytelling—even juggling—are
called art.
This book is about yet another type—
**visual art.**

C

D  Kristen, Liestman Elementary. *My Bedroom.*
Tempera on paper, 18 by 12 inches.

Name the types of visual art in the pictures.
What other types of visual art have you seen?

## Seeing Like an Artist

Which types of art have I learned about?
I could make a list of them in my sketchbook.
I could draw pictures of someone doing each one.
Then I could look back at the pictures to remind me.
Maybe I could even try doing some of them!

Henri Rousseau. *I Myself-Portrait-Landscape*, 1890. Oil on canvas, 39⅜ by 31 inches. National Gallery, Prague, Czech Republic. Art Resource, New York.

# Visual Artists

These pictures show **visual artists.**
They chose art as a **career.**
What type of visual art do you think each of them makes?
What are some other types of visual artists?

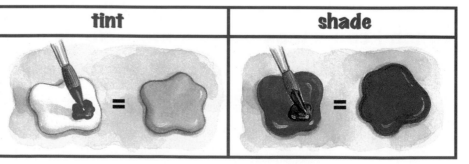

| tint | shade |
|------|-------|
|  | |

 **F** Landry, Woodridge Elementary. *Tints and Shades.* Tempera on paper, 12 by 14¼ inches.

**E** Lee Krasner. *Self-portrait,* 1930. Oil on canvas, 30⅛ by 25⅛ inches. Courtesy Robert Miller Gallery.

Visual artists are often called artists.
The artists in **C** and **E** were painters.
They mixed colors to paint their self-portraits.
They added a color to white to make a **tint.**
They added black to a color to make a **shade.**
You can mix paints to make tints and shades, too.

## Try Your Hand

Imagine that your career is visual art.
Which type of visual artist might you be?
1. Paint a portrait of yourself doing a type of art.
2. Mix paints to make tints and shades.
3. Add details.

# Music and Storytelling

Artist unknown. *Jaguar Man.* Redware pottery. University of Pennsylvania Museum, Philadelphia.

**B**

Some visual artists create artworks about music.
What type of visual artist created **A**?
What tune do you suppose the boy is playing?

A sculptor created **B**.
It is a very old whistle used to make music for dancing.
How is this whistle different from ones you've used?

Artist unknown. *The Preacher*, ca. 1870. Butternut, eastern white pine, 21 by 7½ by 7¼ inches. Abby Aldrich Rockefeller Folk Art Center, Williamsburg, VA.

Veronica, Liestman Elementary. *Tooth Fairy*. Crayon, tempera, glitter, chalk, 18 by 11½ inches.

All people have stories to tell.
What story do you think the preacher might be telling?
What type of visual artist created **C**?

## Planning Like an Artist

I can make an artwork about my favorite story.
First I can tell the story to a friend.
Then I can plan an artwork about it.
I'll make some sketches of my ideas.
I might even write a song to go with my sketches.

*Music and Storytelling* **67**

 Katrina, St. Gregory's School, *Storyteller*. Modeling clay, wood platform, 6½ by 2½ by 4¼ inches.

 Edouard Manet. *The Fifer*, 1866. Oil on canvas, 63½ by 38¼ inches. Musée d'Orsay, Paris, France. Photograph by Erich Lessing/Art Resource, New York.

# Musicians and Storytellers as Subjects

Many artworks have **subjects.**
The subject is the main idea of the artwork.
What are the subjects in these artworks?

Look at the musician in **A**.
What do you notice first?

Look at the storyteller doll in **C**.
Is the adult a lot bigger than the children?
What do you think the sculptor was saying?

Helen Cordero.
*Storyteller*, 1965. Slipped
and painted earthenware,
height 14 inches. From the
Girard Foundation
Collection in the Museum
of International Folk Art, a
unit of the Museum of
New Mexico, Santa Fe,
N. Mex. Photograph by
Michel Monteaux.

**D**

Olivia, Woodridge Elementary.
*Storyteller*. Modeling clay, wood platform,
5 by 4¼ by 2 inches.

Point to the positive space in **A** and **C**.
Where is the negative space?

## Try Your Hand

**What types of storyteller dolls can you imagine?**

1. **Choose a person or an animal as a subject.**
2. **Use modeling clay to make a sculpture of the storyteller.
   Make it large.**
3. **Then make sculptures of the listeners.
   Attach them to the storyteller.**

# Theater and Dance

These **photographs** show people who like to perform.
Some of them are theater performers.
Others are dancers.
Do any of these pictures make you want to perform, too?
Tell why.

E

F

Lines in some photographs give you feelings of **motion.** Look at the pictures. Which movements do you see and feel?

# Thinking Like an Artist

I could think about taking some photographs.
A viewfinder would help me plan.
I could make a viewfinder.
I could practice taking photographs with it.

*Theater and Dance*  71

 Edgar Degas. *Dancers Practicing at the Bar*, ca. 1876-1877. Oil colors freely mixed with turpentine, on canvas, 29¾ by 32 inches. The Metropolitan Museum of Art. Bequest of Mrs. H. O. Havemeyer. The H. O. Havemeyer Collection. 29.100-34.

# Dancers as Subjects

Dancers are a popular subject for paintings.
Some artists paint by watching people dance.
Others paint by using their imaginations.
Still others paint by remembering the way
dancers look and move.

The artist who painted **A** watched the movement
of dancers.
Later he painted the dancers from his sketches
and his memory.

 **72** *Lesson 12*

# How to
## Make a Shadow

1. Cut out the portrait.

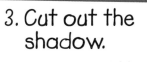

2. Use white chalk and dark paper. Turn the portrait over and draw around it.

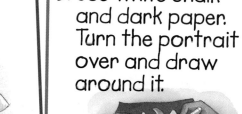

**B** Juan, Zavala Elementary. *Shadow Making.* Construction paper, 9 by 12 inches.

3. Cut out the shadow.

4. Glue the portait and shadow to a lighter background.

**C** Columbia, Zavala Elementary. *The Shadow.* Construction paper, 9 by 12 inches.

Where are the dark colors in **A**?
Where are the light colors?
Point to shadows in **A**.

# Try Your Hand

**Which type of art does your friend like to do?**

1. Watch while your friend pretends to do the type of art she or he likes best.
2. Make a few sketches of your model.
3. Then use crayons to draw your model from your sketches, memory, and imagination. Add details.

**Where will you place your shadow?**

# PORTFOLIO PROJECT

## Festive Vests

Plan with your friends an arts festival.
How will you express your feelings and ideas?
Make a vest to wear that day.

1. Get a large paper sack. Cut it down the center. Make holes for your arms and neck. Cut three slits up each side.

2. Make strips of colored paper and wrapping paper. Weave them over and under through the slits.

3. You can make short sleeves with wrapping paper.

4. Add other details.

Do you like the way you feel in your vest?
Explain why.

# PORTFOLIO GALLERY

**A**

Erica, Wonderland School. *Festive Vest.* Tempera, yarn, paper, 16½ by 6¾ by 12 inches.

**B** Cidnye, Wonderland School. *Festive Vest.* Tempera, yarn, paper, 12 by 6¾ by 14 inches.

# TALK ABOUT ART

**A** William H. Johnson. *Self-portrait*, 1934-1935. Oil on burlap, 26⅛ by 26⅛ inches. National Museum of American Art, Smithsonian Institution, Gift of the Harmon Foundation, Washington, D.C./Art Resource, New York. 1967.59.759.

**B** William H. Johnson. *Jitterbugs I*, ca. 1940-1941. Oil on plywood, 39¾ by 31¼ inches. National Museum of American Art, Washington, D.C./Art Resource, New York.

Look at **A**.
This painting is a self-portrait.
What career do you think the subject chose?
The artist in **A** also painted **B**.

What is happening in **B**?
Point to patterns of lines and shapes.
Name primary and secondary colors in **B**.
How did the painter show movement?
Why do you think he showed the hands
larger than life-size?

 Attributed to Tamura Suio. *Ladies Pastimes in Spring and Autumn*, 18th century. One hand scroll, ink and color on paper, 12⅜ by 96 1/16 inches. Spencer Collection, The New York Public Library. Astor, Lenox and Tilden Foundation.

Point to patterns of lines and shapes in **C**.
Name the primary and secondary colors you see.
Which woman is playing music?
Which one is a visual artist?
Which ones might be practicing lines for a play or reading poetry?

How are **B** and **C** alike?
How are they different?
What do you think each artist was saying?
Would you like to hang **B** on your classroom wall? Explain.
Would you like to have **C** in your room at home? Tell why or why not.

# WRITE ABOUT ART

Look again at **B** on page 76.
The people seem to be having fun.

**Think about a time you had fun with a friend.**
**Write about that time.**
**Tell what you did with your friend.**
**Write about the things that made it fun.**

## Remember:

- Think about what you want to say before you begin.
- Describe how things looked, felt, smelled, tasted, or sounded.
- Use words that tell about your feelings.

# What Have You Learned?

Where have you seen these pictures?

**A** **B** **C**

1. Which subject shows the art of music?
2. Point to the picture that shows a visual artist.
3. What type of art does **C** show?

4. What is the same in all three pictures?
5. Which hands show movement?
6. Point to the artwork called a photograph.
7. What type of visual artist made **A** and **B**?
8. Point to a close-up view of a self-portrait.

9. Turn back to the artwork you would like to show your family. Tell why.
10. Which activities did you enjoy? Explain.
11. What else did you learn about ways of expressing?
12. What artworks or activities would you add to this unit?

Lee Krasner. (Detail) *Self-portrait*, 1930. Oil on canvas, 30⅛ by 25⅛ inches. Courtesy Robert Miller Gallery.

Edouard Manet. (Detail) *The Fifer*, 1866. Oil on canvas, 63½ by 38¼ inches. Musée d'Orsay, Paris, France. Photograph by Erich Lessing/Art Resource, New York.

Diego Rivera. *The Making of a Fresco Showing the Building of a City*, 1931. Fresco, 271 by 357 inches. San Francisco Art Institute. Photograph by David Wakely.

# Sizes of Artworks

Artworks come in many sizes.
Some are very large.
Others are quite small.
Most of them are in between.

Artworks of all sizes appear
in many places.
Look for art on a ceiling.
Discover art that is sunken into the ground.
Notice art painted on walls.
Examine a small piece of jewelry.
You might even find art inside an egg!

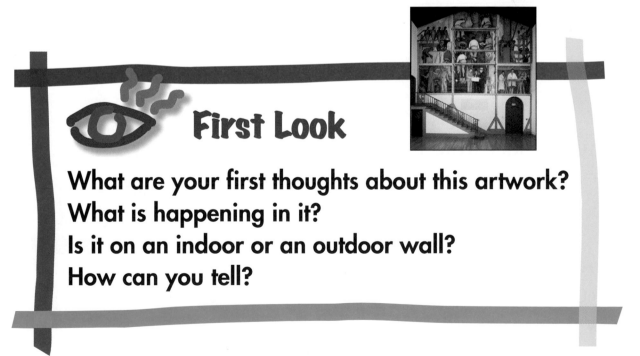

## First Look

What are your first thoughts about this artwork?
What is happening in it?
Is it on an indoor or an outdoor wall?
How can you tell?

# Large Artworks

**A**

**B** Alexander Calder. *Flamingo*, 1973. Steel, 636 by 288 by 720 inches. Federal Center Plaza, Chicago. SuperStock.

Some artists make large **public sculptures.**
Everyone can enjoy these sculptures.

**C**

The artist in **A** made **B**.
Some of his sculptures are taller than trees.
What is the subject of this public sculpture?
How can you tell that **B** is very tall?

 Vito Acconci. *Face of the Earth #3*, 1988. Concrete, approximately 5 by 33 by 29 feet. Collection of Laumeier Sculpture Park, Saint Louis.

You can play on the grass and concrete in **D**.
It is both a large public sculpture and a small park.
What does this sculpture remind you of?

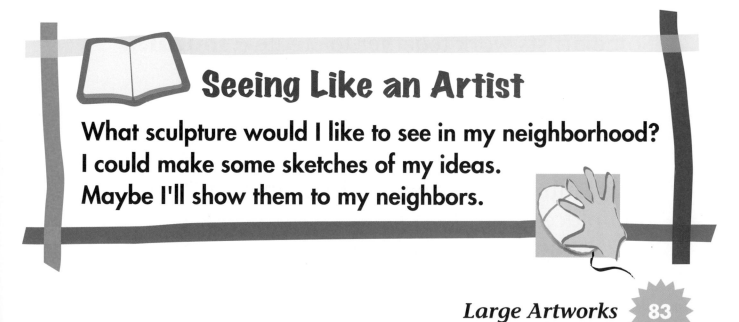

## Seeing Like an Artist

**What sculpture would I like to see in my neighborhood?
I could make some sketches of my ideas.
Maybe I'll show them to my neighbors.**

A

B

# Murals

Some artists work together to create a **mural.**
These **muralists** paint a very large picture.
It's usually on a wall, fence, or ceiling.
The mural often tells a story.

Many murals show **realistic** people, animals, and places.
How would a mural with imaginary subjects look?

# How to
## Create a Mural

1. Plan what the mural is about.
   Make a list of things to be on the mural.

2. Draw or paint the background.

3. Cut out the large shapes you planned.

4. Place them different ways. Talk about which way looks best.

5. Paste them onto the mural.

## Try Your Hand

Work with friends to make a mural about animals.
1. Think of a story for your mural. Will your mural show realistic or imaginary animals?
2. Paint a background for your mural.
3. Cut out shapes and glue them onto the background.

Hang your mural on a wall.

# Small Artworks

Did you ever think a gold palace would fit inside an egg?
Look at **A**.
The egg is only 5 inches tall, yet the palace has 600 rooms!
How would you **display** this artwork for everyone to see?

**A**

Carl Fabergé. *The Gatchina Palace Egg*, 1901.
Enamel, gold, seed pearls, diamonds (at each extremity), 5 by 3 inches. The Walters Art Gallery, Baltimore.

Artist unknown. *Popayan (Columbian) Pectoral,* 1100-1500 A.D. Cast gold-copper alloy, gilded, height 11¾ inches. © The British Museum, London.

**C**

Ben, Campbell Elementary. *Basket of Eggs.* Clay, glaze, 3½ by 3 by 4½ inches.

The small **pendant** in **B** is very old.
Someone long ago wore it as **jewelry.**
Point to different sizes of shapes on the pendant.
Where do you see patterns?
What type of balance did the artist choose?

# Planning Like an Artist

I can plan to sketch jewelry in my sketchbook.
I can sketch from memory, imagination, and by looking.
I'll find things I like by looking through my sketches.
I can use those ideas to make new jewelry designs.

Jonathan, Schertz Elementary. *Tradebeads*. Polyvinylchloride clay, varnish, 10¼ by 5½ inches.

Wayne, Olympia Elementary. *Tradebeads*. Polyvinylchloride clay, varnish, 11 by 6 inches.

Sabrina, Our Lady of Perpetual Help, *Tradebeads*. Polyvinylchloride clay, varnish, 10½ by 5½ inches.

# Tradebeads

Many people around the world have used beads for trade.

They gave a bead and received something in return.

These beads are called **tradebeads.**

Some artists still make tradebeads.

Sometimes friends trade beads to show friendship.

# How to
## Make a Tradebead Necklace

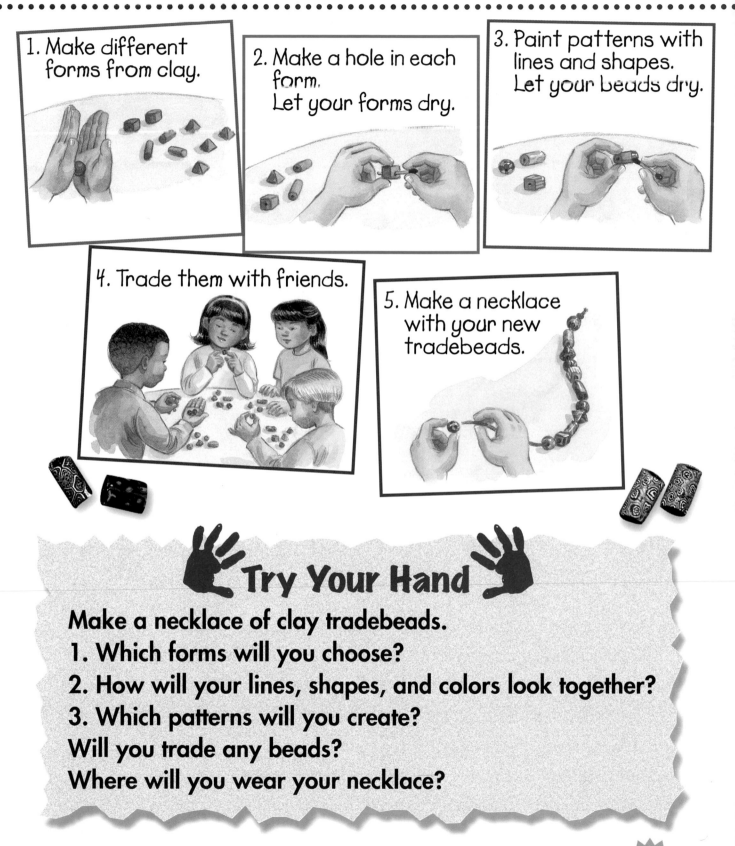

1. Make different forms from clay.

2. Make a hole in each form.
Let your forms dry.

3. Paint patterns with lines and shapes.
Let your beads dry.

4. Trade them with friends.

5. Make a necklace with your new tradebeads.

## Try Your Hand

Make a necklace of clay tradebeads.
1. Which forms will you choose?
2. How will your lines, shapes, and colors look together?
3. Which patterns will you create?
Will you trade any beads?
Where will you wear your necklace?

# Computer Artworks

**A**

**B**

Some artists use computers to plan artworks.
You can find their artworks in many places.
Some are as large as a ceiling.
Others are as small as a book.

**Book designers** work on computers to design books.
These artists plan how each page will look.
They design the way words and photographs fill
space on the pages.
Sometimes they draw illustrations for the book.
Point to a computer design for a book page.

# How to
## Make a Zigzag Book

1. Design a front and a back cover. Let them dry.

2. Fold a long paper to make pages.

3. Cut and paste a computer screen for each page.

4. Write and illustrate your story on the computer screens.

5. Paste the folded paper to the front and back covers.

You can make designs for a book.
You could use the computer as a tool.
What other art tools might you use for your designs?

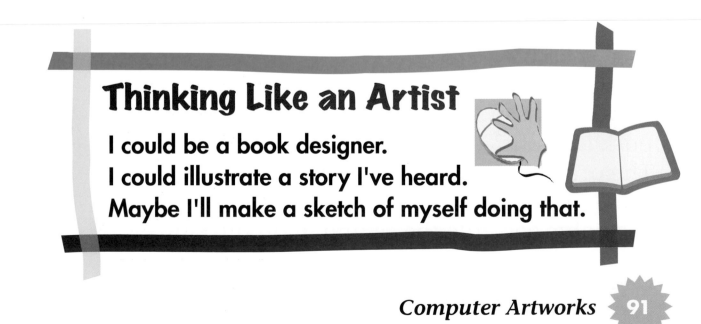

## Thinking Like an Artist

I could be a book designer.
I could illustrate a story I've heard.
Maybe I'll make a sketch of myself doing that.

*Computer Artworks*

Michael Hayden. *Sky's the Limit*, 1991. Neon. Photograph by United Airlines.

# Big Bright Lights

Have you ever seen fireworks exploding in the sky?
Have you seen colored lights in an amusement
park at night?
The artist who created **A** might have seen
these things.
His lights decorate the ceiling in an airport.

A computer turns the lights on and off to the beat of music.
The artist put mirrors above the lights to reflect lines, colors, and movement.
Would you like to visit the walkway below this ceiling? Explain.

## Try Your Hand

Make your own zigzag book.
Look back at page 91 to help you.
Will your cover design look like bright lights?

 Brent, Brannen Elementary. *Zig Zag Book*. Mat board, paper, markers, 31 by 4½ inches.
Jimmy, Forest Trail Elementary. *Zig Zag Book*. Mat board, paper, markers, 42 by 5 inches.
Nick, Our Lady of Perpetual Help. *Zig Zag Book*. Mat board, paper, markers, 49 by 5 inches.
Sabrina, Our Lady of Perpetual Help. *Zig Zag Book*. Mat board, paper, markers, 53¾ by 5 inches.

# PORTFOLIO PROJECT

## Making a Pendant
### Why do people wear jewelry?

1. Cut out a circle, a triangle, and a square. Make them different sizes.

2. Glue them together. Let them dry.

3. Make a hole near the outside edge. Decorate your pendant with markers or paint.

4. Attach your pendant to a necklace.

What kinds of lines and shapes did you make?
Do you like your pendant?
Will you attach it to a tradebead necklace?

# PORTFOLIO GALLERY

Olivia, Eanes Elementary. *Tradebeads with Pendant.* Posterboard, acrylic paint, polyvinylchoride clay, 13 by 6½ inches.

**A**

Philip, Brentwood Elementary. *Tradebeads with Pendant.* Poster board, acrylic paint, polyvinylchoride clay, 14 by 4 inches.

**B**

Layne, Olympia Elementary. *Tradebeads with Pendant.* Poster board, acrylic paint, polyvinylchoride clay, 18 by 6 inches.

**C**

Kelsey, Weiderstein Elementary. *Tradebeads with Pendant.* Poster board, acrylic paint, polyvinylchoride clay, 12 by 6½ inches.

**D**

Nick, Our Lady of Perpetual Help. *Tradebeads with Pendant.* Poster board, acrylic paint, polyvinylchoride clay, 16 by 8 inches.

**E**

*Portfolio Gallery*

# TALK ABOUT ART

A. Frida Kahlo. *Frida and Diego Rivera*, 1931. Oil on canvas, 39⅜ by 31 inches. San Francisco Museum of Modern Art. Albert M. Bender Collection. Gift of Albert M. Bender. Photograph by Ben Blackwell. 36.6061.

B. Diego Rivera. (Detail) *The Making of a Fresco Showing the Building of a City*, 1931. Fresco, 271 by 357 inches. San Francisco Art Institute. Photograph by David Wakely.

The artists in **A** were married to each other.
They lived in Mexico.
What is unusual about their sizes in the portrait?
The woman in **A** painted the portrait.
What do you think she was trying to say?

The man in **A** painted **B**.
What kinds of lines and shapes do you see?
What is each person doing?

 Judy Baca, director; Esabel Castro, designer. (Detail) *1900 Immigrant California, Great Wall of Los Angeles,* 1989-1996. Paint on architectural structures, length approximately 2,640 feet. Photograph by Michael Newman/PhotoEdit.

The mural in **C** is a part of the longest mural in the world. It tells the story of people moving to California.
Students helped paint it.
Is the mural indoors or outdoors? Explain.
Name the different types of lines you see.
Do the people look realistic or imaginary?

Which colors are the same in the murals?
Point to organic and geometric shapes.
What do you think each artist was saying?
Would you like to have the mural in **B** at your school?
Tell why or why not.
Would you like to visit the mural shown in **C**? Explain.

*Unit 5*  97

# WRITE ABOUT ART

Look again at **B** on page 96.
It shows people building a city.
Pretend that you write for the newspaper.
You have some ideas about your city.

Read this list of things you want your city to have.

a new school

an airport

a park

a zoo

Choose one thing from the list.
Write about it for the newspaper.
Tell why it is important for the city.

You might begin your writing with this sentence.

**I think that our city needs a _____ because _____.**

## Remember:

- You want your readers to agree with you.
- You should tell why you feel as you do.

# What Have You Learned?

Where have you seen these pictures?

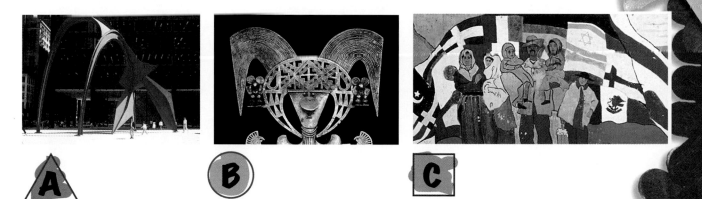

**A**   **B**   **C**

1. Point to close-up views of very large artworks.
2. Point to a close-up view of a very small artwork.
3. Which artwork is a public sculpture?

4. Which two artworks are forms?
5. What type of balance did the artist of **B** choose?
6. Tell about the texture of any two of these artworks.
7. Point to positive space in one of these artworks.
8. Point to negative space.

9. Turn back to the artwork you like best.
10. Which activity was your favorite? Why?
11. Tell about a classmate's artwork.
12. What else did you learn about sizes of artworks?

Alexander Calder. *Flamingo*, 1973. Steel, 636 by 288 by 720 inches. Federal Center Plaza, Chicago. SuperStock.

Artist unknown. (Detail) *Popayan (Columbian) Pectoral*, 1100-1500 A.D. Cast gold-copper alloy, gilded, height 11¾ inches. © The British Museum, London.

Judy Baca, director; Esabel Castro, designer. (Detail) *1900 Immigrant California, Great Wall of Los Angeles*, 1989-1996. Paint on architectural structures, length approximately 2,640 feet. Photograph by Michael Newman/PhotoEdit.

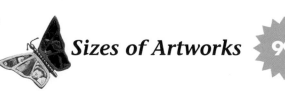

*Sizes of Artworks*

Miriam Schapiro. (Detail) *Master of Ceremonies*, 1985. Acrylic and fabric on canvas, 90 by 144 inches. Collection of Elaine and Stephen Wynn. Courtesy Steinbaum Krauss Gallery, New York. © Miriam Schapiro.

# More Ways of Making Artworks

You've learned about many
ways of making artworks.
Some artists draw, paint, or make prints.
Others create collages, sculpture,
computer art, or photographs.
Still others make jewelry, mosaics,
illustrations, or plans for architecture.
How many more ways could there
be to make art?
You might be surprised to learn that
artists have created in even more ways.
Which ways have you discovered to make art?

## First Look

What is the person in the picture holding?
What type of artwork might this person make?
How does the artwork make you feel? Explain.

# Woven Art

**A**

Hopi People. *Crow Mother*, 1960. Coiled dyed yucca leaf and grass, 12½ inches. From the Girard Foundation, Collection in the Museum of International Folk Art, a unit of the Museum of New Mexico, Santa Fe, N. Mex. Photograph by Michel Monteaux.

The artist of **A** used leaves and grass to make a **weaving.**
Some of the grass was **dyed** to make a design.
Point to patterns on the weaving.
What type of balance did the artist choose?

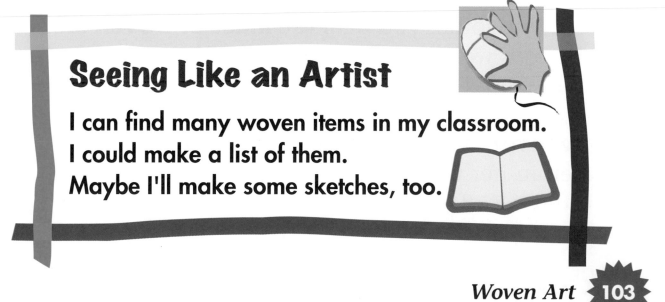

Artist unknown. *Nagapattinam Basket*, 1965. Woven palm leaf with foil, 6½ inches. From the Girard Foundation Collection, in the Museum of International Folk Art, a unit of the Museum of New Mexico, Santa Fe, NM.

People all over the world weave **baskets.**
Have you ever seen a basket like the one in **B**?
Name some textures you might see or feel in **B**.
How is this basket different from others you've seen?
How is it the same?
What would you keep inside this basket?

## Seeing Like an Artist

I can find many woven items in my classroom.
I could make a list of them.
Maybe I'll make some sketches, too.

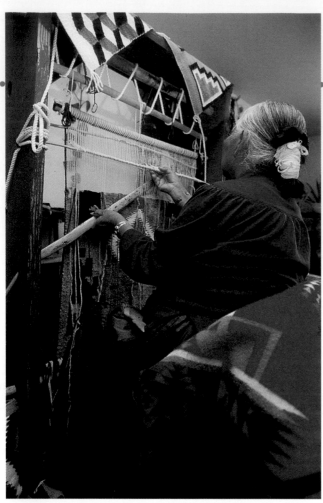

Kelsey, Weiderstein Elementary. *Straw Weaving.* Yarn, beads, feathers, 2¾ by 13 inches.

Barrett, Olympia Elementary. *Straw Weaving.* Yarn, beads, 4½ by 11 inches.

# Weaving Fibers to Make Cloth

Name a **fabric** that you like to wear.
Most of the clothes you wear are made of **woven** fabrics.
The threads were woven over and under on a **loom.**
What else have you seen that is woven?

The **weaver** in **A** is weaving a blanket on a loom.
Women in her village have woven in this way
for hundreds of years.
Each one taught another to weave.

1. Cut five strips of thick yarn. Push them through five soda straws. Tie knots in one end of each strip.

2. Tie the other ends together.

3. Weave over and under. Weave back and forth. Do it again and again.

4. Cut the small knots. Pull the straws out.

What have you learned from other people?
What have you taught others?

## Try Your Hand

You can learn to weave a bookmark.
1. What colors of yarn will you use?
2. What details will you add to your bookmark?
3. Will you use your weaving in your zigzag book?

# Art for Celebrations

**A**

**B**

Artist unknown (Cameroon). *Large Dance Headdress,*
19th century. Wood, height 26½ inches. Werner
Forman Archive, Fuhrman Collection, New York.
Photograph © Art Resource, New York.

Some artists make art for celebrations.
They make things like hats and
other **headdresses.**
Each headdress has special meaning.

The wooden headdress in **B** is more than 2 feet tall.
How would it feel to dance with it on your head?
The patterns were made by carving into the wood.
Talk about the textures you see and feel.

**C**

How do the headdresses in **C** differ from those
in **A** and **B**?
Would you like to wear one of these headdresses?
Explain.

## Planning Like an Artist

I'll plan to go to the library.
I can learn about what people wear to celebrate.
I'll make some sketches about what I learn.

*Art for Celebrations*

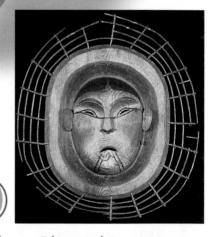

Artist unknown. *Jaguar Mask*, 1960. Painted wood, height 9½ inches. From the Girard Foundation Collection in the Museum of International Folk Art, a unit of the Museum of New Mexico, Santa Fe, N. Mex. Photograph by Michel Monteaux.

# Masks

Have you ever worn a **mask**?
Why did you wear it?
How did it make you feel?

Artist unknown. *Eskimo Mask Representing a Moon Goddess*, 19th century. Wood, spruce root bindings, fish skin tie, 25¹⁷⁄₃₂ by 22¼ inches. Phoebe A. Hearst Museum of Anthropology, University of California at Berkeley.

Masks often help people celebrate.
They can change the way people look and feel.

# How to
## Make a Sack Mask

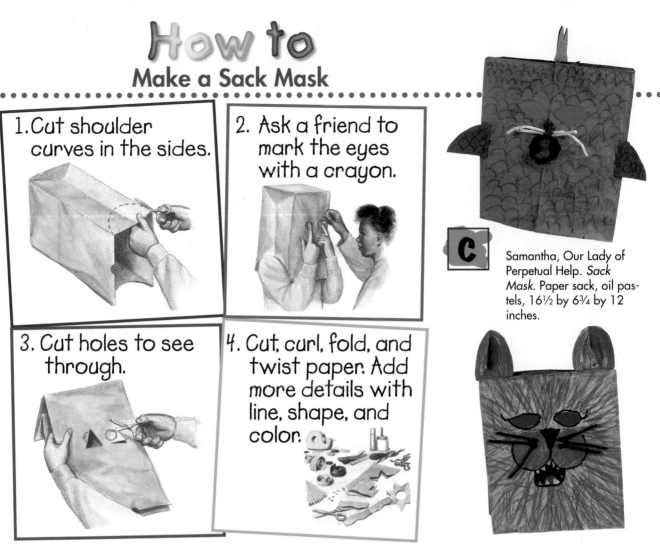

1. Cut shoulder curves in the sides.

2. Ask a friend to mark the eyes with a crayon.

3. Cut holes to see through.

4. Cut, curl, fold, and twist paper. Add more details with line, shape, and color.

**C** Samantha, Our Lady of Perpetual Help. *Sack Mask.* Paper sack, oil pastels, 16½ by 6¾ by 12 inches.

**D** Rickey, Our Lady of Perpetual Help. *Sack Mask.* Paper sack, oil pastels, 16½ by 6¾ by 12 inches.

Tell about the balance of **A** and **B**. How do the lines, shapes, and colors go together to make patterns?

## Try Your Hand

1. Talk with some friends about a favorite celebration.
2. Write a short play about it together.
3. Use your imagination to create a mask for your play.
4. Perform the play with your group.
How do the masks look together?

# Art in Everyday Places

 Mierle Laderman Ukeles. *The Social Mirror*, 1983. Mirror-covered garbage truck with the New York City Department of Sanitation. Courtesy Ronald Feldman Fine Arts, Inc., and the Department of Sanitation, City of New York.

Can you imagine a garbage truck as an artwork? The artist of **A** planned this artwork in honor of garbage collectors.

She wanted to show her thanks for the job they do.

The people could see themselves in the mirrors.

The mirrors reminded them of the need to recycle.

Ave Bonar. *Man Pushing Grocery Carts*, 1974. Black and white photograph.
Courtesy of the artist.

The photographer of **B** saw space filled in an unusual way.

She saw an unusual design in an ordinary place.

What is unusual about **B**?

Point to interesting lines in the photograph.

What patterns do you see?

Can you feel the movement?

## Thinking Like an Artist

I can think of many ordinary places and things.
I see them every day.
I'll make some sketches of something ordinary,
but I'll show it in a new and unusual way.

## Signs and Symbols

Signs help us understand what is around us.
Symbols on signs often take the place of words.
Look around your neighborhood and find
signs with symbols.
Artists design signs with symbols.
These designs show words in pictures.
What do the symbols in **A**, **B**, and **C** mean?
Tell about other signs in your neighborhood.
How do they help you every day?

# How to
## Make a Sign Rubbing

1. Choose a message for your sign. Draw symbols for your message.

2. Cut and paste colored paper. Start with the largest shape. End with the smallest shape.

3. Let it dry. Cover it with newsprint. Rub over it with the side of a crayon.

4. Display both pictures.

**D**

**E** Michael, Ed White Elementary. *I Love Trees.* Construction paper, crayons, newsprint, 15 by 18 inches.

## Try Your Hand

Imagine a sign that needs to be made.

1. Think of a symbol for your sign.

2. Make a rubbing of it.

Where would you like to see your sign posted?

## Weaving Patterns

How could you use a paper weaving?
Could it be an ornament, a wall hanging, or a
background for another artwork?

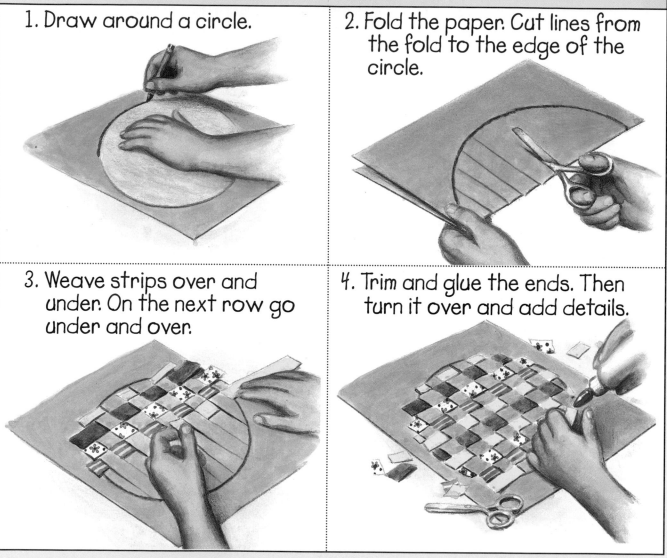

1. Draw around a circle.

2. Fold the paper. Cut lines from the fold to the edge of the circle.

3. Weave strips over and under. On the next row go under and over.

4. Trim and glue the ends. Then turn it over and add details.

Which colors did you choose?
What pattern does your weaving show?
Where will you display your woven pattern?

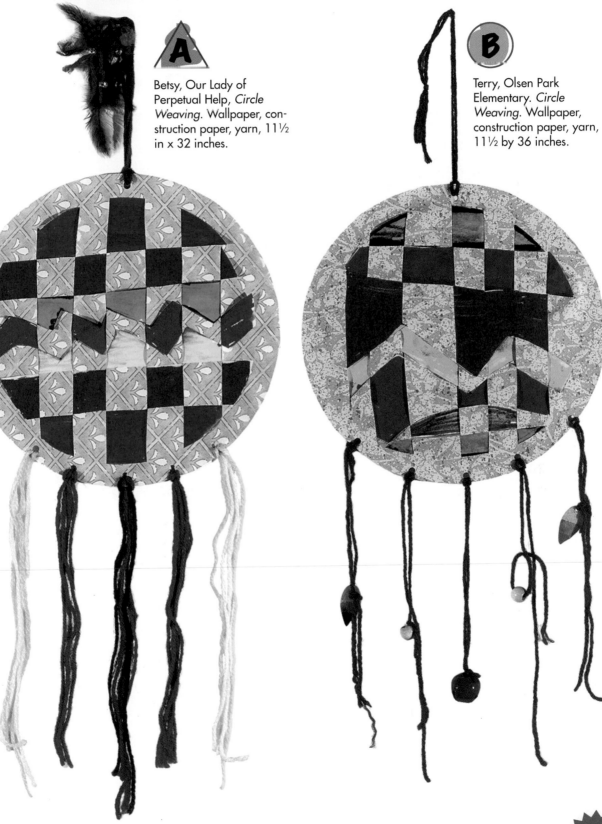

**A**

Betsy, Our Lady of Perpetual Help, *Circle Weaving*. Wallpaper, construction paper, yarn, 11½ in x 32 inches.

**B**

Terry, Olsen Park Elementary. *Circle Weaving*. Wallpaper, construction paper, yarn, 11½ by 36 inches.

# TALK ABOUT ART

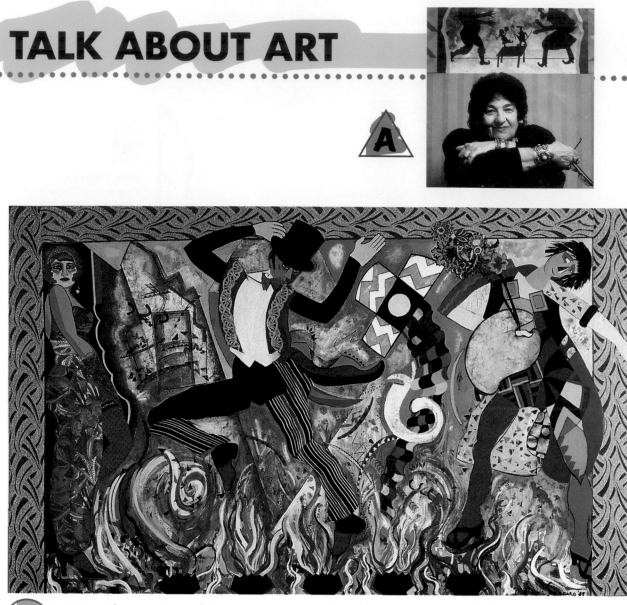

 Miriam Schapiro. *Master of Ceremonies*, 1985. Acrylic and fabric on canvas, 90 by 144 inches. Collection of Elaine and Stephen Wynn. Courtesy Steinbaum Krauss Gallery, New York. © Miriam Schapiro.

The artist in **A** created **B**.
She made **B** with paints and beautiful recycled fabrics.

How did the artist make her artwork feel warm?
Where do you see movement?
Find patterns of line, shape, and color.
What is happening in this artwork?

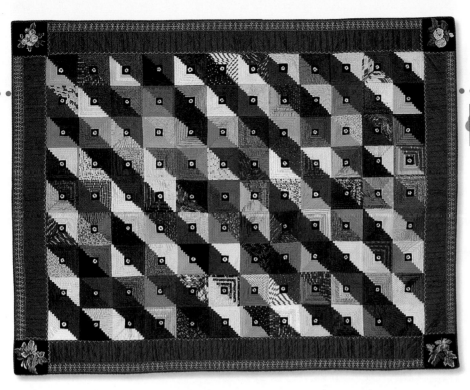

Artist unknown. *Log Cabin*, late 19th century. Coverlet, silk, handmade patchwork, 80 by 63 inches. Courtesy of The Witte Museum, San Antonio.

Why do you think **C** is called a log cabin **quilt**?
Older quilts like this one were usually made by groups of women.
They **sewed** together **blocks** to make the quilt design.
What types of clothing might have been recycled into this quilt?
How do you think the quilt was used long ago?
Why is it in a museum today?

How are **B** and **C** alike?
How are they different?
Which artwork was designed to be used?
Which one was made to be displayed?

Would you like to see **B** in a museum?
Tell why or why not.
Would you like to have a log cabin quilt made for you? Explain.

# WRITE ABOUT ART

Look again at **B** on page 116.
The artist shows many things happening at once.

Write to someone who has not seen the artwork.
Tell about the colors you see.
Tell something about the patterns.
Then choose one person in the artwork.
Write about what this person is doing.
Add something about how the person looks.

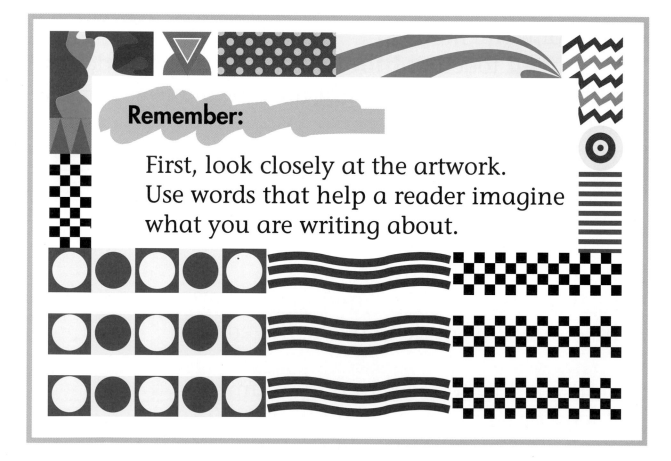

**Remember:**

First, look closely at the artwork.
Use words that help a reader imagine
what you are writing about.

# What Have You Learned?

Where have you seen these pictures?

 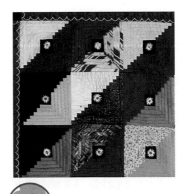 

 **A**     **B**     **C**

1. Which picture shows a quilt block?
2. How was the quilt block made?
3. How was this quilt probably used?

4. Point to a loom.
5. What type of artwork is made on a loom?
6. Name some types of weavings.

7. Where is a close-up view of a mask?
8. What details do you notice in the mask?

9. Turn back to the artwork you like best. Tell why.
10. Did you especially enjoy an activity? Why?
11. Which of your own artworks pleases you most? Why?
12. What else did you learn about more ways of making artworks?

Artist unknown. (Detail) *Jaguar Mask*, 1960. Painted wood, height 9½ inches. From the Girard Foundation Collection in the Museum of International Folk Art, a unit of the Museum of New Mexico, Santa Fe, N. Mex. Photograph by Michel Monteaux.

Artist unknown. (Detail) *Log Cabin*, late 19th century. Coverlet, silk, handmade patchwork, 80 by 63 inches. Courtesy of The Witte Museum, San Antonio.

*More Ways of Making Artworks*

# Think Safety

Look at the pictures on these pages.
They show children using art materials safely.

Then read the safety rules.
Follow these rules when you make artworks.

1. **Keep art materials away from your mouth.**

2. **Keep art materials away from your eyes.**

3. **Do not breathe chalk dust or art sprays.**

4. **Look for the word nontoxic on labels. This means the materials are safe to use.**

5. Always use safety scissors.
   Take care with all sharp objects.

6. Use only new meat trays and egg cartons.

7. Wash your hands when you finish an artwork.

8. If you have a problem, get help from your teacher.

 Can you think of more ways to be safe?

# Picture Glossary

**architect**
Page 30

**architecture**
Page 31

**assemblage**
Page 44

**balance**
Page 50

**basket**
Page 103

**block (quilt)**
Page 117

**book designer**
Page 90

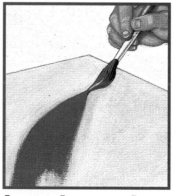

**brush stroke**
Page 7

**career**
Page 64

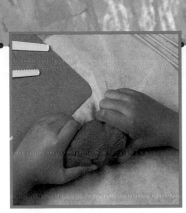

**clay**
Page 48

**collage**
Page 24

**cool colors**
Page 12

**design**
Page 48

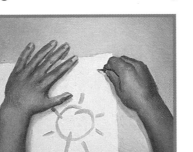

**display**
Page 86

**dye**
Page 102

**express**
Page 26

**fabric**
Page 104

**forms**
Page 31

**headdress**
Page 106

**imaginary**
Page 11

**jewelry**
Page 87

**kiln**
Page 49

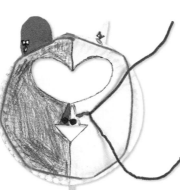

**lines**
Page 2

**loom**
Page 104

**mask**
Page 108

**model** (for an artwork)
Page 28

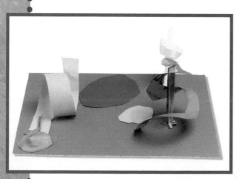

**model** (of a playscape)
Page 30

**mosaic**
Page 50

**motion**
Page 71

**movement**
Page 4

**mural**
Page 84

**muralist**
Page 84

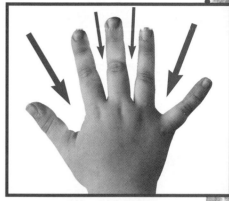

**negative space**
Page 42

**painting**
Page 7

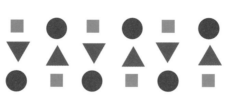

**pattern**
Page 22

**pendant**
Page 87

**photograph**
Page 70

**playscape**
Page 32

**portrait**
Page 28

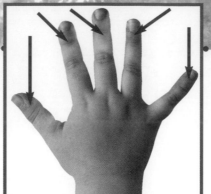

**positive space**
Page 42

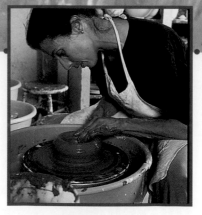

**potter**
Page 48

**pottery**
Page 48

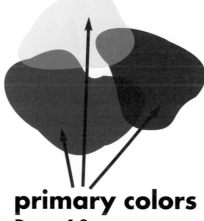

**primary colors**
Page 10

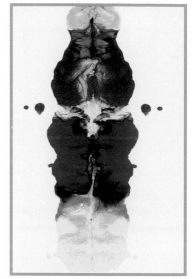

**print**
Page 23

**printing stamp**
Page 34

**public sculpture**
Page 82

**puppet**
Page 47

**realistic**
Page 84

**quilt**
Page 117

**radial balance**
Page 51

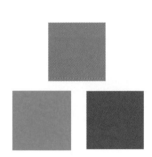

**sculpture**
Page 42

**secondary
colors**
Page 10

**self-portrait**
Page 29

**shapes**
Page 3

**sew**
Page 117

**space**
Page 6

**stencil**
Page 52

**symmetrical balance**
Page 50

**texture**
Page 6

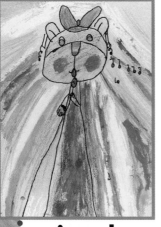

**visual art**
Page 62

**visual artist**
Page 64

**warm colors**
Page 12

**weaver**
Page 104

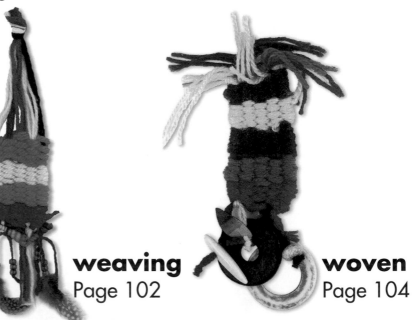

**weaving**
Page 102

**woven**
Page 104

# Index

# ACKNOWLEDGMENTS

## CONTRIBUTORS

*The author and publisher wish to thank the following teachers for their contributions to the development of ideas and procedures for art activities and projects in this series:*

Martha Camacho, Wanza Coates, Joan Elder, Kelly Fox, Lisa Fuentes, Maureen Clare Gillis, Karen Johnson, Joan Klasson, Leisa M. Koch, Lara Landers, Tamera S. Moore, Sharon R. Nagy, Teri Evans-Palmer, Julie Pohlmann, Jean Powell, Cynde Riddle, Nancy J. Sass, Lori Schimmel, Melissa St. John, Sue Telle, Susan Urband, Fatima Usrey, Pamela Valentine, Caryl E. Williams

*We appreciate the efforts of the following teachers who graciously submitted student art for use in this series:*

Wanza Coates, Linda Caitlin, Joan Elder, Kelly Fox, Karen Johnson, Joan Klasson, Dottie Myers, Julie Pohlmann, Jean Powell, Dana Reyna, Nancy J. Sass, Lori Schimmel, Ingrid Sherwood, Melissa St. John, Tammy Suarez, Marie Swope, Sue Telle, Susan Urband, Fatima Usrey, Marilyn Wylie, Jamie Wood

*We wish to thank the following teachers for their expertise, wisdom, and wholehearted good will during the field testing of this series:*

Sammie Gray, Mary Alice Lopez, Robin Maca, Deborah McLouth, Lois Pendley, Dana Reyna, Ingrid Sherwood, Sue Telle, Marilyn Wylie

*We gratefully acknowledge the following schools for allowing us to work with their teachers and students during the development of this series:*

Conley Elementary, Aldine Independent School District; Roosevelt Elementary, San Antonio Independent School District; Amelia Earhart Learning Center, Dallas Independent School District; Cedar Creek Elementary, Eanes Independent School District; Smith Elementary, Alief Independent School District; Heflin Elementary, Alief Independent School District; Hill Elementary, Austin Independent School District; Odom Elementary, Austin Independent School District; Brooke Elementary, Austin Independent School District; Campbell Elementary, Austin Independent School District; Zavala Elementary, Austin Independent School District; Langford Elementary, Austin Independent School District; Brentwood Elementary, Austin Independent School District; Burnet Elementary, San Antonio Independent School District; Edgewater Elementary, Anne Arundel County Public Schools; Landis Elementary, Alief Independent School District; Boone Elementary, Alief Independent School District; College of Fine Art, Maryland Institute, Baltimore, Maryland; Orange Grove Elementary, Aldine Independent School District; Klentzman Intermediate School, Alief Independent School District; Forest Trail Elementary, Eanes Independent School District; Teague Middle School, Aldine Independent School District; Bethune Academy, Aldine Independent School District; Martin Elementary, Alief Independent School District; Petrosky Elementary, Alief Independent School District; North Hi Mount Elementary, Fort Worth Independent School District; Cambridge Elementary, Alamo Heights Independent School District; Porter Elementary, Birdville Independent School District; Woodridge Elementary, Alamo Heights Independent School District; Anderson Academy, Aldine Independent School District; Creative Fine Arts Magnet School, San Francisco Unified School District; Wonderland School, San Marcos, Texas; Olsen Park Elementary, Amarillo Independent School District; Liestman Elementary, Alief Independent School District; Hogg Elementary, Dallas Independent School District; Bivins Elementary, Amarillo Independent School District; Tuckahoe Elementary, Arlington Public Schools, Fine Arts Department of North East Independent School District; Fox Hill Elementary, Indianapolis Public Schools.

A special acknowledgment to the founders of the SHARE program in San Antonio, Texas, Pamela Valentine and Sue Telle, who graciously allowed us to share with the world their prized and inspirational student artwork. The SHARE (Students Help Art Reach Everyone) program is a foundation dedicated to students and their art, and develops opportunities for students to interact with and enlighten their community.

*A final acknowledgment to Barrett and Kendall, the inspiration behind State of the Art.*

# PHOTO CREDITS

Key: (t) top, (c) center, (b) bottom, (l) left, (r) right.

**UNIT 1.** Page xii, 16(tr), © 1998 Artists Rights Society (ARS), New York/VG Bild Kunst, Bonn.; 2, 6(t), 18, Barrett Kendall photo by Andrew Yates; 11(t), © 1998 Artists Rights Society (ARS), New York/ADAGP, Paris; 12, Photograph by Giraudon/Art Resource, NY; 13, 19(tr), Photograph © 1996 The Metropolitan Museum of Art; 16(tr) © 1998 Artists Rights Society (ARS), New York/VG Bild Kunst, Bonn.; 19(tr), photograph © 1996 The Metropolitan Museum of Art.

**UNIT 2.** Page 22(tl), Photo ©Robyn M. Turner; 22(c), 25(tr), SuperStock; 25 (tl), © 1996 Succession H. Matisse, Paris/Artists Rights Society (ARS), New York; 26(tr), Barrett Kendall photo by Peter Van Steen; 32(t/vertical), 32(l), 39(r), Tony Freeman/PhotoEdit; 32(r), Richard Hutchings/PhotoEdit; 37 Artwork ©1983 Melissa Miller.

**UNIT 3.** Page 44(tl), Gay Block; 51(l), Texas Department of Commerce/Tourism; 56(l), UPI/Bettmann.

**UNIT 4.** Page 62(tr), Photo ©Robyn M. Turner; 62(l), 62(c), Barrett Kendall photo by Andrew Yates; 63(l), Photo ©Robyn M. Turner; 64(tl), 64(cl), Michael Newman/PhotoEdit; 66(l), 70(tl), 70(c), 70(r), 70(b), 71(l), 71(r), 79(r), Texas Department of Commerce/Tourism; 66(r), Neg. # T4-796; 72, Photograph © 1986 The Metropolitan Museum of Art.

**UNIT 5.** Page 82(tl), Dominique Berretty/Black Star; 82(br), E. Manewal/SuperStock; 84(t), F.B. Grunzweig/Tony Stone Images; 84(c), Tony Freeman/PhotoEdit; 84(br), E.R. Degginger/Bruce Coleman, Inc.; 88(t), David Young-Wolff/PhotoEdit; 88(l), Holton Collection/SuperStock; 90, Barrett Kendall photo by Andrew Yates.

**UNIT 6.** Page 104, Paul Conklin/PhotoEdit; 106(tl), Photo ©Robyn M. Turner; 106(tr), Werner Forman/Art Resource, New York; 107, Texas Department of Commerce/Tourism; 112(t), Grant Faint/The Image Bank; 112(l), Tom Prettyman/PhotoEdit; 112(r), Hildegard Adler; 116, Sebastian Piras, 1994, Courtesy Steinbaum Krauss Gallery, NYC; 119(r), Paul Conklin/PhotoEdit.

Page 120-121, Barrett Kendall photos by Andrew Yates; 122(first row, 2nd), Texas Department of Commerce/Tourism (bl) Barrett Kendall photo by Andrew Yates,(br) Michael Newman/PhotoEdit; 123(tl) Barrett Kendall photo by Andrew Yates, (third row,l) Barrett Kendall photo by Peter Van Steen; 124(first row,2nd) Barrett Kendall photo by Andrew Yates, (second row,l) Paul Conklin/PhotoEdit, (br)Barrett Kendall photo by Peter Van Steen; 125(tl) F.B. Grunzweig/Tony Stone Images, (second row, left) Tony Freeman/PhotoEdit, (bl) Barrett Kendall photo by Peter Van Steen, (br) Richard Hutchings/PhotoEdit.

© Photodisc, Inc. pages, i-iv background; vi, vii, viii, ix, x, xi(br), 1, 6(tr, mr), 7(br), 8(br), 12(m), 13(tr), 21(tr), 30(br), 32(t), 39(b), 41(m), 43(b), 58, 61(t), 79(b), 81(t), 103(tr), 124(tl), 127(tl, b), 128(tr)

# ILLUSTRATION CREDITS

**Holly Cooper:** 14, 26, 33, 53, 72, 73, 74, 78, 85, 89, 91, 127, 128

**David Fischer:** 49, 53, 71, 94, 105, 109, 114, 123

**Doug Henry:** 122, 123, 126

**Mike Jarowski:** 123, 124, 128

**Mike Krone:** 7, 11, 23, 34, 56, 98, 113, 126

**132** *Acknowledgments*